LIFE STORY

ANT

MICHAEL CHINERY

Photography by
Barrie Watts

Illustrated by
Nichola Armstrong

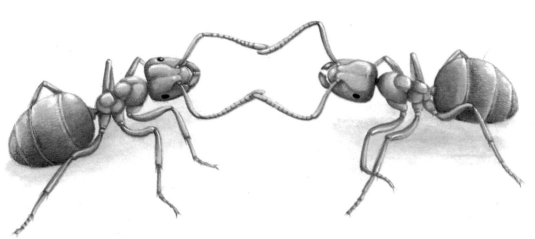

Troll Associates

Library of Congress Cataloging-in-Publication Data

Chinery, Michael.
    Ant / by Michael Chinery; photography by Barrie Watts;
illustrated by Nichola Armstrong.
      p.   cm.—(Life story)
    Summary: An introduction to the physical characteristics, habits,
and natural environment of various types of ants.
    ISBN 0-8167-2098-3 (lib. bdg.)   ISBN 0-8167-2099-1 (pbk.)
    1. Ants—Juvenile literature. [1. Ants.] I. Watts, Barrie,
ill. II. Armstrong, Nichola , ill. III. Title. IV. Series:
Chinery, Michael. Life story.
QL568.F7C54 1991
595.79′6—dc20   90-10947

Published by Troll Associates

Designed by James Marks

Printed in the U.S.A.

10 9 8 7 6 5 4 3

INTRODUCTION

Ants are amazing creatures that live and work together in large colonies. Each ant seems to know exactly what it has to do for the good of the whole colony. In this book you will discover how the ants look after their eggs and grubs, and how the grubs eventually turn into adult ants. You will also find out how the ants collect food and how they get sugary honeydew by stroking aphids. You will also discover the reason for the swarms of flying ants that annoy people so much on certain days in the summer.

The ant in the picture is a meadow ant. She is looking for food. She will take anything she finds back to her nest, where she lives with thousands of other ants. Each nest, or colony, has one or more queens, but nearly all the ants are workers like the one in the photograph. All worker ants are female. As well as collecting food, the worker ants build the nest and keep it clean.

They also look after the eggs and young ants, and they have to feed the queens regularly. The queens are much bigger than the workers because their bodies are full of eggs.

4

Meadow ants live in grassy places, where they build anthills up to three feet (one meter) high. Each hill is made of soil, which the ants dig from the ground below. The anthill is full of rooms and hallways, and there are more rooms underground.

Some rooms are used as nurseries for the eggs and baby ants, while others are used as stables for the aphids that provide the ants with much of their food.

The ants in the picture are busy working at one of the nest entrances, although meadow ants don't actually go out very much. They spend most of their time underground.

The queen ant does nothing but lay eggs. She lays many thousands of eggs during her life. The worker ants gather them up as soon as she has laid them.

The ants in the picture are piling eggs into one of the nurseries. You can see the ants' toothy jaws very clearly. They can give you a nasty bite, but they are very gentle with their eggs.

The nurseries are usually near the surface of the anthill, where the sun's warmth helps the eggs to develop quickly.

The nest of these ants has been damaged, and the workers in the picture are rushing around to gather up the eggs that have been scattered. They will carry the eggs deep into the nest, where they will be safe until the workers can rebuild the mound.

The eggs are very valuable to the ants, and the workers spend a lot of time turning them over and licking them clean. The eggs soon get moldy if they are not kept clean in this way.

The eggs hatch a few days after they are laid and produce the legless white grubs or larvae that you can see in the picture. The workers are licking the grubs to keep them clean.

Newly hatched grubs eat some of the unhatched eggs around them until the workers start bringing food for them. For the first few days, the grubs receive a liquid food coughed up by the workers. Later on, the workers bring them pieces of insects to eat.

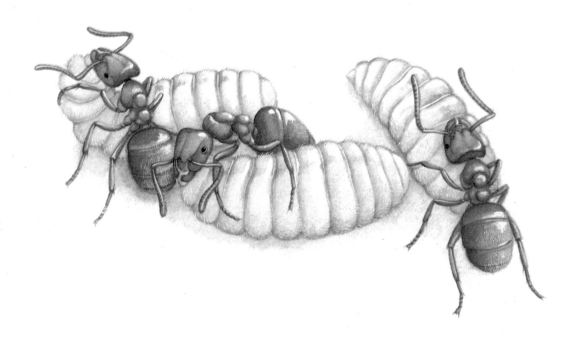

Ant larvae get hairier as they grow up. The one in the picture is nearly fully grown and will soon be ready to turn into an adult ant. A worker ant is carrying it to another part of the nest.

During the summer, when the weather is warm, the ant larvae take only a week or two to grow up, but larvae that hatch in the fall don't grow up until the following spring. They spend the winter huddled together in clusters deep in the nest, out of reach of the frost.

14

When the ant larva is fully grown, it spins a sausage-shaped cocoon around itself, using silk from its own body. The worker ants pile up the cocoons in the warmest part of the nest, as you can see in the photograph.

Although the cocoons are larger than the workers, they are not very heavy. The workers can easily carry them in their jaws. Ant cocoons are often sold as food for goldfish, although they are usually called ants' eggs.

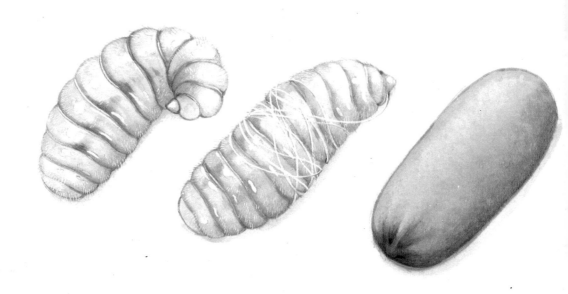

18

Inside its cocoon, the ant larva begins the wonderful change to the adult insect. First it shrugs off its old skin and becomes a pupa. One of the cocoons in this photograph has been cut open to show the pupa.

It looks like an adult ant from the outside, but things are still going on inside it to change the larval body into that of an adult. Notice that there are two sizes of cocoon in the picture. The big ones contain developing queens, while the others contain worker ants.

Worker ants guard the cocoons and listen for movements telling them that the new ants are ready to come out. The workers then bite open the cocoons and help the new ants to climb out.

As you can see in the photograph, the new ants are very pale. They are also very soft, but their skins soon harden. Then the ants are ready for work.

They stay in the nest for the first few weeks, looking after eggs and grubs. Then they go out to hunt for food in the surrounding soil.

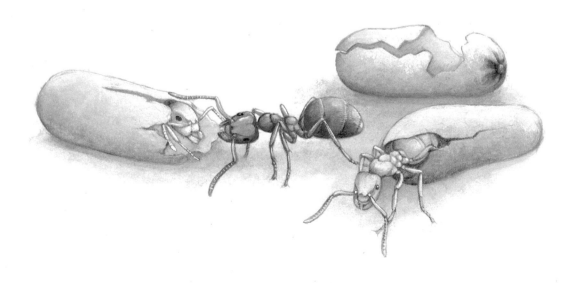

Meadow ants spend most of their time hunting in the soil, where they catch beetles, mites, and other small animals. They even eat other ants. Sometimes they hunt above ground.

The ant in the photograph has found a caterpillar. The caterpillar is too big for one ant to manage, but other meadow ants will soon come along to help. They will overpower the caterpillar and cut it up with their jaws. Then they will drag the pieces back to the nest and feed them to the grubs.

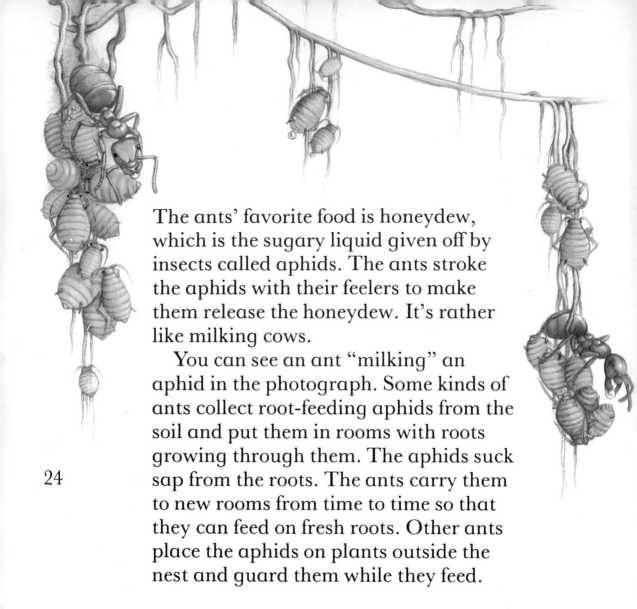

The ants' favorite food is honeydew, which is the sugary liquid given off by insects called aphids. The ants stroke the aphids with their feelers to make them release the honeydew. It's rather like milking cows.

You can see an ant "milking" an aphid in the photograph. Some kinds of ants collect root-feeding aphids from the soil and put them in rooms with roots growing through them. The aphids suck sap from the roots. The ants carry them to new rooms from time to time so that they can feed on fresh roots. Other ants place the aphids on plants outside the nest and guard them while they feed.

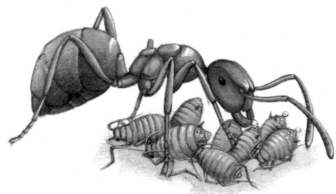

These ants look as if they are fighting, but they are actually passing food to each other. This is a very important part of life in the ant colony.

When an ant finds a good supply of honeydew or other food, she brings some back and gives little pieces to other workers. This excites them, and they go out to look for the food themselves. In this way, the ants bring back as much as possible to feed to the grubs and the other ants in the nest.

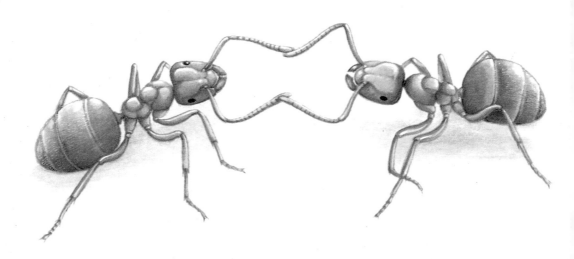

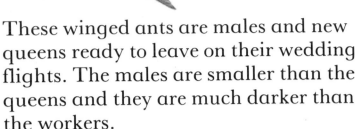

These winged ants are males and new queens ready to leave on their wedding flights. The males are smaller than the queens and they are much darker than the workers.

Huge swarms of flying ants leave the nests in August. The ants mate in the air and then fall to the ground. The males die soon after this, but the queens have busy lives ahead of them. Each one breaks off her wings and makes her way into a nest. She will live for ten years or more, laying thousands of eggs every year. Many of the eggs produce new queens which start new nests of their own, and so the cycle begins all over again.

28

Fascinating facts

Weaver ants, which live in warm countries, make small nests by gluing leaves together. The glue is a sticky kind of silk which is given out by the ant grubs when they are squeezed.

Ants often have guests in their nests. As well as the aphids that they keep to provide them with honeydew, there are many beetles and small white woodlice that feed on tiny scraps and help to keep the nest clean.

Weaver ants

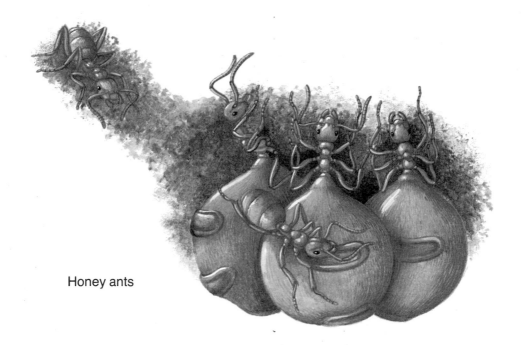

Honey ants

Some ants actually keep slaves to do some of their work. They go out from time to time and steal cocoons from the nests of other kinds of ants, and when the workers emerge from these cocoons they settle down to work in the nests of their captors.

In some parts of the world there are ants called honey ants and some of their workers act as living honey pots. They hang from the walls of the nest and fill themselves with nectar and honeydew brought by the other workers. Their bodies swell up to an enormous size, and in bad weather the other workers come to them to get a drink of honey.

Index